Let's Read About Our Bodies

Feet

by Cynthia Klingel* and Robert B. Noyed
photographs by Gregg Andersen

*Amoroso is preferred name

Reading Consultant: Cecilia Minden-Cupp, Ph.D.,
Adjunct Professor, College of Continuing and Professional Studies, University of Virginia

WeeklyReader.
EARLY LEARNING LIBRARY

For a free color catalog describing Weekly Reader® Early Learning Library's list of high-quality books, call 1-800-542-2595 or fax your request to (414) 332-3567.

Library of Congress Cataloging-in-Publication Data

Klingel, Cynthia.
    Feet / by Cynthia Klingel and Robert B. Noyed.
      p. cm. — (Let's read about our bodies)
    Includes bibliographical references and index.
    Summary: A simple introduction to feet and their features.
    ISBN 0-8368-3064-4 (lib. bdg.)
    ISBN 0-8368-3153-5 (softcover)
    1. Foot—Juvenile literature. [1. Foot.] I. Noyed, Robert B. II. Title.
    QM549.K54   2002
    612'.98—dc21   2001054990

This edition first published in 2002 by
Weekly Reader® Early Learning Library
330 West Olive Street, Suite 100
Milwaukee, WI 53212 USA

Copyright © 2002 by Weekly Reader® Early Learning Library

An Editorial Directions book
Editors: E. Russell Primm and Emily Dolbear
Art direction, design, and page production: The Design Lab
Photographer: Gregg Andersen
Weekly Reader® Early Learning Library art direction: Tammy Gruenewald
Weekly Reader® Early Learning Library production: Susan Ashley

Printed in the United States of America

1 2 3 4 5 6 7 8 9 06 05 04 03 02

Note to Educators and Parents

As a Reading Specialist I know that books for young children should engage their interest, impart useful information, and motivate them to want to learn more.

Let's Read About Our Bodies is a new series of books designed to help children understand the value of good health and taking care of their bodies.

A young child's active mind is engaged by the carefully chosen subjects. The imaginative text works to build young vocabularies. The short, repetitive sentences help children stay focused as they develop their own relationship with reading. The bright, colorful photographs of children enjoying good health habits complement the text with their simplicity and both entertain and encourage young children to want to learn — and read — more.

These books are designed to be used by adults as "read-to" books to share with children to encourage early literacy in the home, school, and library. They are also suitable for more advanced young readers to enjoy on their own.

— Cecilia Minden-Cupp, Ph.D.,
Adjunct Professor, College of Continuing and
Professional Studies, University of Virginia

These are my feet!

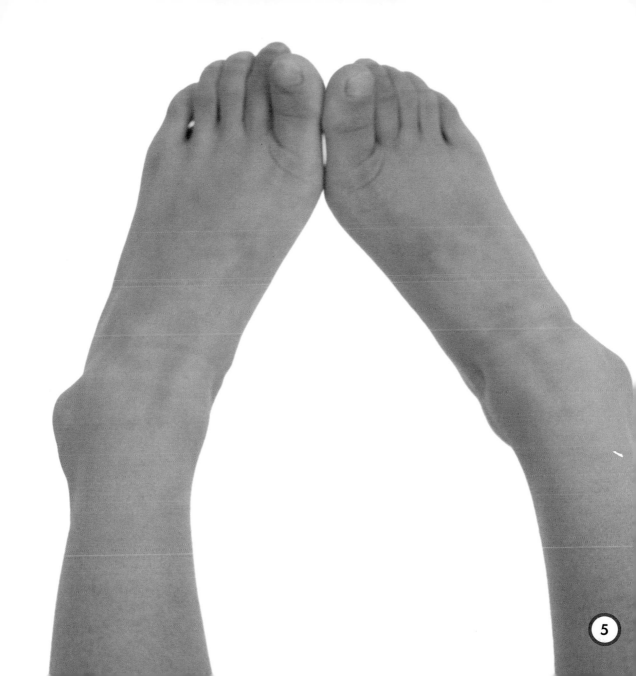

I have two feet.

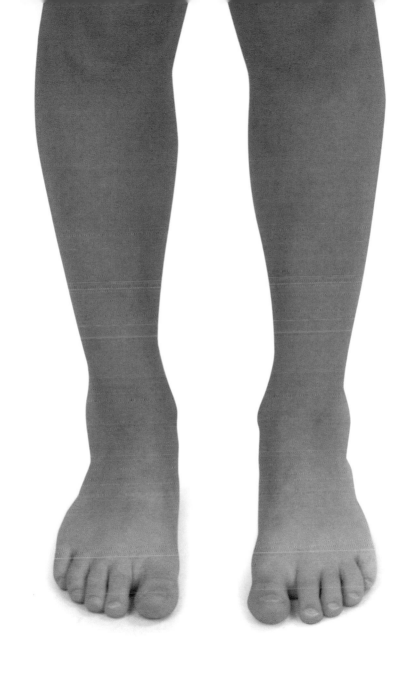

7

My feet are small.
Some feet are big.

My feet help me walk and run.

I have ten toes.
I can wiggle my
toes. Can you?

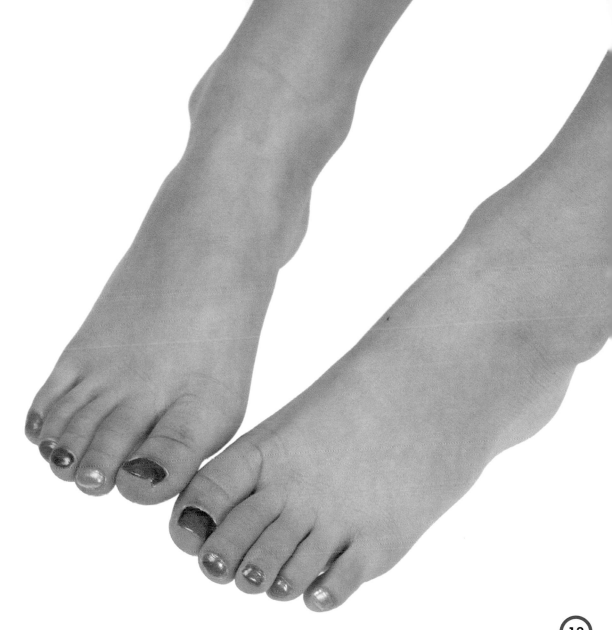

I keep my toenails short and clean.

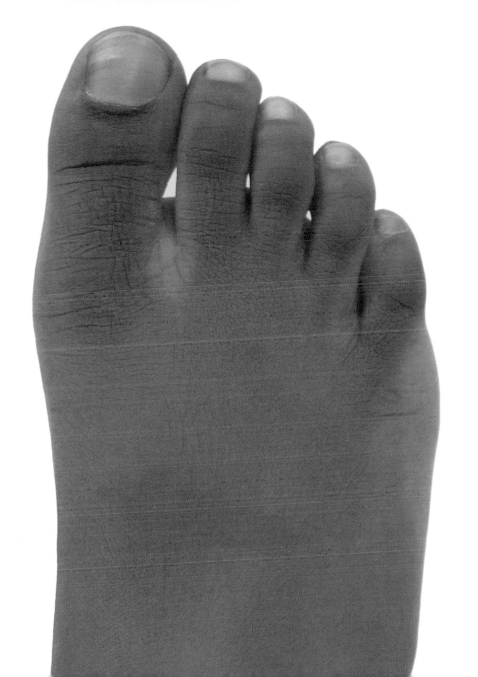

I keep my feet warm. I wear socks.

I keep my feet safe.
I wear shoes.

Feet are fun to tickle!

Glossary

tickle—to touch the body in a way that causes a tingling feeling

toenails—a thin, hard layer of material growing at the end of each toe

wiggle—to move from side to side in short, sudden movements

For More Information

Fiction Books

Hamm, Diane Johnson. *How Many Feet in the Bed?* New York: Simon and Schuster, 1991.

Paul, Ann Whitford. *Hello Toes! Hello Feet!* New York: DK Publishing, 2000.

Rau, Dana Meachen. *Feet.* Danbury, Conn.: Children's Press, 2000.

Nonfiction Books

Cromwell, Sharon. *Why Do My Feet Fall Asleep?* Chicago: Heinemann Library, 1998.

Swanson, Diane. *Up Close: Feet That Suck and Feed.* New York: Greystone Books, 2000.

Yagyu, Genichiro. *The Soles of Your Feet.* New York: Kane/Miller Books, 1997.

Web Sites

Why Does My Foot Fall Asleep?

kidshealth.org/kid/talk/qa/foot_asleep.html

For information about sleepy feet

Index

About the Authors

Cynthia Klingel has worked as a high school English teacher and an elementary school teacher. She is currently the curriculum director for a Minnesota school district. Cynthia Klingel lives with her family in Mankato, Minnesota.

Robert B. Noyed started his career as a newspaper reporter. Since then, he has worked in school communications and public relations at the state and national level. Robert B. Noyed lives with his family in Brooklyn Center, Minnesota.